MW01030825

The Adventure Begins

_____

_____

Table of Contents

PAGE #	DESTINATION	TRAVEL DATES	DISTANCE

Destination:

_____
_____

Travel Dates:

Distance:

Weather:

Sites to see:

_____
_____
_____
_____
_____

Best experiences of the trip:

_____
_____
_____
_____
_____
_____
_____
_____
_____

Lessons learned for next time:

_____
_____
_____
_____
_____
_____
_____
_____
_____
_____

Photos & Memorabilia

Destination:

_____

_____

Travel Dates:

Distance:

Weather:

Sites to see:

_____

_____

_____

_____

_____

Best experiences of the trip:

Lessons learned for next time:

Photos & Memorabilia

Destination:

_____

_____

Travel Dates:

Distance:

Weather:

Sites to see:

_____

_____

_____

_____

_____

Best experiences of the trip:

_____

_____

_____

_____

_____

_____

_____

_____

_____

_____

_____

Lessons learned for next time:

_____

_____

_____

_____

_____

_____

_____

_____

_____

_____

_____

Photos & Memorabilia

Destination:

_____

_____

Travel Dates:

Distance:

Weather:

Sites to see:

_____
_____
_____
_____
_____
_____

Best experiences of the trip:

_____
_____
_____
_____
_____
_____
_____
_____
_____
_____

Lessons learned for next time:

_____
_____
_____
_____
_____
_____
_____
_____
_____
_____

Notes & Memories

Photos & Memorabilia

Destination:

_____

_____

Travel Dates:

Distance: 🌐🏠🧭🪧

Weather: ☀️🌧️❄️🌡️

Sites to see: 📍🏢📷🗺️

_____
_____
_____
_____
_____

Best experiences of the trip:

_____
_____
_____
_____
_____
_____
_____
_____
_____

Lessons learned for next time:

_____
_____
_____
_____
_____
_____
_____
_____

Notes & Memories

Photos & Memorabilia

Destination:

Travel Dates:

Distance:

Weather:

Sites to see:

Best experiences of the trip:

Lessons learned for next time:

25

Photos & Memorabilia

Destination:

_____

_____

Travel Dates:

Distance:

Weather:

Sites to see:

_____
_____
_____
_____
_____
_____

Best experiences of the trip:

_____
_____
_____
_____
_____
_____
_____
_____
_____
_____

Lessons learned for next time:

_____
_____
_____
_____
_____
_____
_____
_____
_____
_____

Photos & Memorabilia

Destination:
_____
_____

Travel Dates:

Distance:

Weather:

Sites to see:

Best experiences of the trip:

Lessons learned for next time:

_____
_____
_____
_____
_____
_____
_____
_____
_____
_____
_____

Photos & Memorabilia

Destination:

_____
_____

Travel Dates:

Distance:

Weather:

Sites to see:

_____
_____
_____
_____
_____

Best experiences of the trip:

_____
_____
_____
_____
_____
_____
_____
_____
_____

Lessons learned for next time:

_____
_____
_____
_____
_____
_____
_____
_____
_____

Photos & Memorabilia

Destination:

_____

_____

Travel Dates:

Distance:

Weather:

Sites to see:

_____
_____
_____
_____
_____

Best experiences of the trip:

_____
_____
_____
_____
_____
_____
_____
_____
_____
_____

Lessons learned for next time:

_____
_____
_____
_____
_____
_____
_____
_____
_____
_____

Photos & Memorabilia

Destination:

_____
_____

Travel Dates:

Distance:

Weather:

Sites to see:

_____
_____
_____
_____
_____

Best experiences of the trip:

Lessons learned for next time:

Photos & Memorabilia

Destination:

_____

_____

Travel Dates:

Distance:

Weather:

Sites to see:

_____

_____

_____

_____

_____

Best experiences of the trip:

_____

_____

_____

_____

_____

_____

_____

_____

_____

Lessons learned for next time:

_____

_____

_____

_____

_____

_____

_____

_____

_____

Notes & Memories

Photos & Memorabilia

Destination:

_____

_____

Travel Dates:

Distance:

Weather:

Sites to see:

_____

_____

_____

_____

_____

Best experiences of the trip:

_____

_____

_____

_____

_____

_____

_____

_____

_____

_____

Lessons learned for next time:

_____

_____

_____

_____

_____

_____

_____

_____

_____

_____

_____

Photos & Memorabilia

Destination:

_____

_____

Travel Dates:

Distance:

Weather:

Sites to see:

_____
_____
_____
_____
_____
_____

Best experiences of the trip:

_____
_____
_____
_____
_____
_____
_____
_____
_____
_____
_____

Lessons learned for next time:

_____
_____
_____
_____
_____
_____
_____
_____
_____
_____

Notes &
Memories

Photos & Memorabilia

Destination:

_____

_____

Travel Dates:

Distance:

Weather:

Sites to see:

_____
_____
_____
_____
_____
_____

Best experiences of the trip:

_____
_____
_____
_____
_____
_____
_____
_____
_____
_____
_____

Lessons learned for next time:

_____
_____
_____
_____
_____
_____
_____
_____
_____
_____

Notes &
Memories

Photos & Memorabilia

Destination:

_____
_____

Travel Dates:

Distance:

Weather:

Sites to see:

_____
_____
_____
_____
_____
_____

Best experiences of the trip:

_____
_____
_____
_____
_____
_____
_____
_____
_____
_____

Lessons learned for next time:

_____
_____
_____
_____
_____
_____
_____
_____
_____
_____

Photos & Memorabilia

Destination:

_____

_____

Travel Dates:

Distance:

Weather:

Sites to see:

_____
_____
_____
_____
_____
_____

Best experiences of the trip:

_____
_____
_____
_____
_____
_____
_____
_____
_____
_____
_____

Lessons learned for next time:

_____
_____
_____
_____
_____
_____
_____
_____
_____
_____

Notes &
Memories

Photos & Memorabilia

Destination:

_____

_____

Travel Dates:

Distance:

Weather:

Sites to see:

_____
_____
_____
_____
_____
_____

Best experiences of the trip:

_____
_____
_____
_____
_____
_____
_____
_____
_____

Lessons learned for next time:

_____
_____
_____
_____
_____
_____
_____
_____
_____

Photos & Memorabilia

Destination:

_____

_____

Travel Dates:

Distance:

Weather:

Sites to see:

_____

_____

_____

_____

_____

Best experiences of the trip:

_____

_____

_____

_____

_____

_____

_____

_____

_____

Lessons learned for next time:

_____

_____

_____

_____

_____

_____

_____

_____

_____

Notes & Memories

Photos & Memorabilia

Destination:
_____
_____

Travel Dates:

Distance:

Weather:

Sites to see:
_____
_____
_____
_____
_____
_____

Best experiences of the trip:
_____
_____
_____
_____
_____
_____
_____
_____
_____
_____

Lessons learned for next time:
_____
_____
_____
_____
_____
_____
_____
_____
_____
_____

Photos & Memorabilia

Destination:

_____
_____

Travel Dates:

Distance:

Weather:

Sites to see:

_____
_____
_____
_____
_____

Best experiences of the trip:

_____
_____
_____
_____
_____
_____
_____
_____
_____
_____

Lessons learned for next time:

_____
_____
_____
_____
_____
_____
_____
_____
_____
_____

Photos & Memorabilia

Destination:

_____

_____

Travel Dates:

Distance:

Weather:

Sites to see:

_____

_____

_____

_____

_____

_____

Best experiences of the trip:

_____

_____

_____

_____

_____

_____

_____

_____

_____

Lessons learned for next time:

_____

_____

_____

_____

_____

_____

_____

_____

_____

Photos & Memorabilia

Destination:

_____

_____

Travel Dates:

Distance:

Weather:

Sites to see:

_____

_____

_____

_____

_____

Best experiences of the trip:

_____

_____

_____

_____

_____

_____

_____

_____

_____

_____

Lessons learned for next time:

_____

_____

_____

_____

_____

_____

_____

_____

_____

Photos & Memorabilia

Destination:

_____
_____

Travel Dates:

Distance:

Weather:

Sites to see:

_____
_____
_____
_____
_____
_____

Best experiences of the trip:

Lessons learned for next time:

Photos & Memorabilia

Destination:

_____
_____

Travel Dates:

Distance:

Weather:

Sites to see:

_____
_____
_____
_____
_____

Best experiences of the trip:

_____
_____
_____
_____
_____
_____
_____
_____
_____
_____

Lessons learned for next time:

_____
_____
_____
_____
_____
_____
_____
_____
_____
_____

Notes & Memories

Photos & Memorabilia

Destination:

_____

_____

Travel Dates:

Distance:

Weather:

Sites to see:

_____

_____

_____

_____

_____

Best experiences of the trip:

_____

_____

_____

_____

_____

_____

_____

_____

Lessons learned for next time:

_____

_____

_____

_____

_____

_____

_____

_____

Photos & Memorabilia

Made in United States
Orlando, FL
29 January 2023

29178619R00061